PILLAR BOXES

Jonathan Glancey

PILLAR BOXES

Chatto & Windus

LONDON

Published in 1989 by
Chatto & Windus Ltd
30 Bedford Square
London WC1B 3SG

A CIP catalogue record for this book
is available from the British Library.

ISBN 0 7011 3447 X

Photoset and printed in Great Britain by
Redwood Burn Limited, Trowbridge, Wiltshire

CONTENTS

PREFACE

This book is a small testament to a pillar of public service, in the hope that some future privatisation scheme may not destroy a treasured and efficient national institution in the vainglorious pursuit of spurious modernisation and mindless profit.

I would not have been able to write it without the help and kindness of Jean Young Farrugia and the staff of the Post Office Archives, Peter Hale at the Post Office Photographic Collection, and the education department of the Design Council.

JONATHAN GLANCEY
North West London Letter District 1989

INTRODUCTION

The red British pillar box is a familiar public servant – perhaps all too familiar. Do we take it too much for granted? Asked to imagine or draw a pillar box, most people would come up with an identical response: a smooth red hollow cast iron pillar or column rising from a black circular base, topped off with a broad fluted cap. A gaping wide-lipped mouth, a firmly locked door and a royal coat of arms would add the finishing touches.

But give the pillar box a second thought, and you will realise that it comes in dozens of different shapes and sizes, if not colours – though there have been ignominious experiments with yellow boxes, and there were once special blue boxes for the early air mail service. Yet, painted in their standard uniform of scarlet and black, like guardsmen standing on point duty, British pillar boxes have been made to look as much like one another as possible. Because of this, the pillar box is one of the few remaining examples of an instantly recognisable public utility.

Whatever the economic pros and cons of privatisation in the 1980s, companies like British Telecom have destroyed forever the idea of dignified, uniform design for what is euphemistically called 'street furniture', which includes telephone kiosks and pillar boxes. Today it is difficult to spot one of the banal and anonymous new telephone kiosks, but the red pillar box remains unmistakable. Peer down any street or lane for a place to post your letters and the GPO pillar box makes itself known, loud and clear.

The privateers' desire to make everything look as fashionable, as different and as temporary as possible has been most fully realised in

London. Only a few years ago London's scarlet double decker buses, telephone kiosks and pillar boxes made an unrivalled ensemble. It was quite clear from appearances alone that public services were working in harmony, and were there to enhance the efficient working as well as the appearance of the city. Within a decade the ruthless pursuit of profit has given London streets the aspect of some provincial Third World town. The idea of good civic design is considered anathema.

Like the handsome red telephone kiosks designed by the architect Sir Giles Gilbert Scott in the 1920s and 1930s, pillar boxes are small works of *architecture*. As you would expect of a design that we have inherited from the mid nineteenth century, pillar boxes draw their inspiration from classical architecture. Early free-standing boxes included designs that adopted the style of the Tower of the Winds from ancient Greece, while others were in the guise of squat fluted Greek Doric columns. This association between Greek civilisation and letter-writing was a noble one. The importance of the mail was fully recognised in the design of these roadside monuments. The standard boxes that we know so well today date from as long ago as 1879. For years they complemented the old GPO telephone kiosks; today that special relationship between post and telecommunications has been destroyed, and our streets have been the poorer for it.

The Post Office has experimented with new designs for pillar boxes yet, fortunately, most design work has been put into refining what already exists. There was a short period of concern in 1968 when the GPO began erecting a new slab-sided rectangular design by the Sheffield cutlery designer David Mellor. The first of these brutally functional post boxes was put up outside the great west front of St Paul's Cathedral. It was neither popular nor tough enough for the job.

Another, much more successful, attempt to redesign the pillar box followed in 1979. After much discussion about new designs in modern plastics, it was a relief to discover that the new model, designed by Tony Gibbs, was a proper pillar box, cast traditionally in iron and painted scarlet and red. This, the Type K box of 1979, is spreading slowly through British streets, but only when and where a new box is needed or where an old one finally succumbs to fatigue. Pillar boxes last a long time – some are well over a hundred years old – but like any hard-worked man-made artefact they eventually give up the ghost. The K type is a welcome newcomer, and adds to the wealth of British pillar box design.

Not everyone has loved the pillar box. G. K. Chesterton thought that 'In all created nature there is not perhaps anything so completely ugly as a pillar box.' In 1909 Chesterton had some useful suggestions for redesigning the National Standard pillar box:

> If the old Greeks had had such an institution, one may be sure that it would have been surmounted by a severe, but graceful, figure of the god of letter writing. If the medieval Christians has possessed it, it would have had a niche filled with the golden aureole of St Rowland of the Postage Stamps. In after years we may have perhaps a pillar box carved with figures emblematical of the secrets of comradeship and the silence and honour of the state.

Others, however, have loved the object of Chesterton's scorn – and none more so than the onetime Postmaster-General, Anthony Wedgwood Benn, who has a very old one in his garden. In his preface to Jean Young Farrugia's scholarly tome *The Letter Box* Benn recalled that 'From boyhood my favourite one has been a wall box on Ocea Island in the River Blackwater in Essex. There is a causeway connecting the island to the mainland which is deeply submerged at high water. Along that causeway the postman used to cycle to the empty box which was – and still is – marked with the unusual inscription "Collection According To The Tide".' It is hard to imagine that particular box surviving some future privatisation scheme.

Yet the Ocea Island letter box is not the most remote. Throughout the old Empire and Commonwealth, British pillar boxes are to be found in regular use. Arabs and Israelis alike pop letters into British pillar boxes, stripped of their royal coats of arms, in Jerusalem, Haifa and Tel Aviv. Victorian examples survive in the hill towns of the Himalayas, in Gibraltar, and throughout Australia and New Zealand. If you began spotting British pillar boxes your hobby would take you right round the world. Being a much-loved British institution, the pillar box naturally has its fan clubs.

This book can only hope to give an outline guide to the complexities of pillar box history and pillar box design. But if it encourages you to delve further, then you must contact the Letter Box Study Group, which is always pleased to hear from anyone with fresh information on curious, forgotten or threatened pillar boxes.

PILLAR BOXES

From Post To Pillar

The state postal service was given over to public use by Charles I in 1635. This was not done as a munificent public gesture, but, perhaps inevitably, to raise revenue to pay for the Royal Mail. The mail service at this point was a hit-and-miss affair, and the famous Mail Coach service which gave Britain its first credible and reliable postal delivery service had to wait until 1784.

Although Mail Coaches were the Inter City 125s of their day, their carrying capacity was extremely limited. The supply of fresh crews and horses needed on the long gallop from London to Scotland, dodging highwaymen on the way, was inevitably an expensive affair, and the cost of mailing a letter was correspondingly high. Letters were charged according to the number of miles they had to travel and it was really only the wealthy who could indulge in long-distance letter-writing.

A letter sent from London to Edinburgh in Charles I's reign cost 9d and took, on a good day, about eighty-five hours to reach its destination. The 'Letter Office' created in 1635 was charged with carrying mail at a regulation speed of seven miles per hour in summer and five miles per hour in winter, so that 'any man may with safetie and securitie send letters to any part of this Kingdom, and receive an answer within five days.' Although this sounds as much as one can expect of the postal service three hundred and fifty years on, it must be added that bad weather and treacherous roads often made the going a lot slower than this regal promise.

The Post Office proper was set up in 1660 by Charles II. Until then management of the post had been handled by the highest bidder, an early form of Thatcherism that was clearly considered unsatisfactory. A penny post system was established within London in 1680 by the enterprising William Dockwra, but this service was taken over by the Crown two years later. Penny post services followed in other major towns and cities, but progress was slow, Edinburgh and Dublin not adopting the idea until as late as 1773, while rapidly expanding industrial towns such as Liverpool and Manchester hung on until the early years of the nineteenth century.

The mail service between towns was greatly improved by the arrival of the Mail Coach service in 1784. All coaches began and ended their journey at the General Post Office in London. By 1835 one of the most popular daily spectacles in London was watching the simultaneous departure of the twenty-eight Royal Mail coaches as they galloped into the night, destined for all points of the compass. Changing horses every ten miles, they were able to average nine miles per hour, which cut the journey from London to Edinburgh from eighty-five hours to sixty. Each coach was protected from highwaymen by a heavily-armed guard. The Mail Coaches finally disappeared in 1846, when the London to Norwich coach handed its mantle to the steam trains of the Great Eastern Railway.

Before the great postal reforms instigated by Sir Rowland Hill in 1840, the gathering and distribution of mail was still very much a random affair, despite the efficiency of the Mail Coaches themselves. At this time there were post masters in each major settlement, but many worked on an amateur basis, including the Lake poet William Wordsworth, who made considerable use of the early mail services himself. Rapid industrialisation forced a change of pace as local penny post services were launched, but the need for instant communication across the country and to and from the ever-receding outposts of the British Empire made a comprehensive and universal postal system a necessity rather than a luxury by the time Queen Victoria ascended the throne.

Rowland Hill's Penny Post was established at long last in 1840

Decorative lady, decorative pillar box:
'Brussels-style' box first seen in Paris, as
depicted in this line drawing from the
Illustrated London News in 1850. (*Post
Office*)

and the pillar box – as well as the domestic letter box – followed soon after. The need for the roadside pillar box was immediately apparent. Post masters were obviously unwilling to receive mail over the counter after-hours, while a spate of fireworks hurled down letter openings in early post offices suggested a need for sturdy iron boxes sited on the roadside. Such boxes already existed in various flamboyant architectural guises in France, Germany and Belgium – the first generation of French roadside letter boxes dates from as early as 1635.

However, the pillar box was preceded by the letter box set flush into the wall of local post offices. These were standardised only after 1912, when James Ludlow of Birmingham won a contract to supply a large proportion of these steel-framed wooden boxes. The same contractor was able to hold on to this commission, producing just two designs, until 1965, when the firm closed down.

The pillar box itself made its first appearance in St Helier in the Channel Islands. Its introduction followed a report written by the future novelist Anthony Trollope, who was then employed as the Clerk to the Surveyor of the South Western District of the Post Office, one of the six postal districts that had been set up in 1715. Trollope wrote that

> There is at present no receiving office in St Helier. Postage stamps are sold in every street and therefore all that is wanted is a safe receptacle for letters ... iron posts suited for the purpose may be erected at the corner of streets in such situations as may be desirable, or probably, it may be found more serviceable to fix iron letter boxes about five feet from the ground, wherever permanently built walls, fit for the purpose, can be found.

Trollope's report was acted on quickly and John Vaudin, a St Helier blacksmith, was commissioned to cast the first seven pillar boxes in 1852. No trace of the drawings he worked to survives, nor is there any indication of who actually designed the first pillar box. However, one of these handsome and instantly recognisable boxes

ROAD-SIDE
LETTER BOXES.

Notice to the Public.

On and after the 23rd Nov., Road-side Letter Boxes will be opened for collecting the public corespondence in the following situations :—

DAVID PLACE,
Nearly opposite the Rectory.

NEW STREET,
In front of Mr. Ivry's, Painter and Glazier.

CHEAPSIDE,
Top of the Parade.

ST. CLEMENT's ROAD,
Corner of Plaisance.

The Letter Boxes will be cleared daily (Sundays excepted) at the following periods, until further notice :

SIX A. M. AND AT NOON,

Except on Mail-days, when, instead of at Noon, they will be cleared as soon as the Packet is signalled.

Letters deposited in these Boxes will be disposed of in all respects in the same manner as if posted at the Principal Office, previous to the above-named period.

Post-office, St. Helier, November, 1852.

PRINTED AT "THE JERSEY TIMES" OFFICE, LIBRARY-PLACE.

Notice of November 1852 announcing the arrival of the letter box in St Helier, Jersey. (*Crown Copyright*)

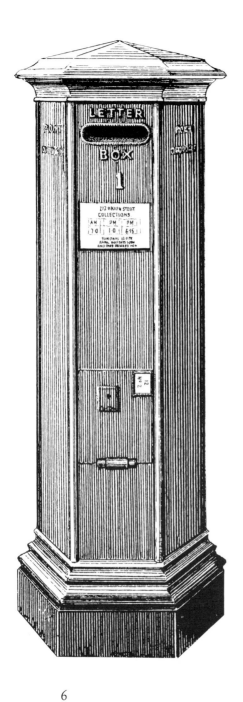

Contemporary line drawing of what is meant to be the very first pillar box erected in Union Street, St Peter Port, Guernsey, 1853, although it could be a replacement dating from 1854–9. (*Crown Copyright*)

still survives (numbered 'One', it is possibly the very first pillar box of all) in use in Union Street, St Peter Port, Guernsey.

These first hexagonal pillar boxes were four feet eight inches high, with a horizontal posting mouth or aperture, and were painted red and adorned with William IV's royal cipher. Letters fell into the base of the box, but bags suspended within the boxes soon followed, while wire guards were installed in all pillar boxes from 1859, to prevent letters from falling onto the street when the boxes were opened for collection. The only complaints concerned not the design of these new intrusions in the high street, but the fact that they were too small, and too few and far between.

Trollope's experiment was considered a huge success, and the pillar box was exported quickly to mainland Britain. The very first to be cast by Messrs Abbott and Co was installed at Botchergate, Carlisle, in 1853. Yet no fixed design had yet been agreed: local district surveyors were able to make their own decisions in terms of both manufacture and design, so the earliest boxes might be hexagonal or octagonal, they might have vertical or horizontal mouths (although the horizontal mouth was officially approved from 1859), they might be quite plain or else, as those cast by Smith and Hawke's Eagle Foundry Birmingham, in the guise of Greek Doric columns. The Eagle Foundry boxes, designed by a local architect whom we know only as Mr Edge, were remarkable objects, standing no less than eight feet tall and topped off with an elongated dome surmounted by a giant, ornate crown. In fact they were extremely expensive to make and an embarrassment to the Post Office. One found a home at Birmingham New Street station for many years, but, sadly, has long since vanished.

Smith and Hawkes, however, met with greater success with a smaller fluted Doric pillar box, examples of which were installed as far afield as Kent and Hampshire. Nevertheless, most early boxes displayed a commendable economy of form – quite out of character, in fact, with the period in which they appeared, then at the height of the Gothic Revival. Quite clearly letter-writing and the post were

Pillar hat, pillar box. Postman poses beside early mainland box.
Windsor, c.1857. (*Post Office*)

associated with learning and education which, in Victorian Britain, were based firmly on the values, culture and literature of classical civilisation. Perhaps this was why the Gothic style was never adapted for use by the designers of pillar boxes.

That the Goths never got their hands on the design of standard pillar boxes was perhaps a lucky thing. Partly because pillar boxes always looked so functional, they were never pilloried by modern designers and architects, who might otherwise have used their influence during the middle of the twentieth century to have them uprooted and replaced with slab-sided iron boxes.

Curiously enough, the first post boxes to be erected in London were rather primitive when compared to those established by Trollope in the Channel Islands. Designed by E. A. Cowper, Consulting Engineer to the Post Office, and made by Messrs H. & M. D. Grissell of Hoxton, they were little more than rectangular iron boxes, five feet tall, capped with a shallow domed roof and crowned with a large iron ball. The first six were installed in Fleet Street, the Strand, Pall Mall, Piccadilly, Grosvenor Place and Knightsbridge.

London's first boxes proved to be unsatisfactory. The low-set notices carrying instructions could be read by pedestrians only if they stooped down, and were plastered with mud and manure on rainy days. Critics were also quick to point out the aesthetic limitations of Cowper's unfortunate design. In an editorial, *The Builder* decried the 'absence of that guiding artistic power which the country has had and still has in its own pay and command if the government chose to avail itself of such service.'

Such complaints gave rise to consultation between the Post Office and the government's Department of Science and Art based in South Kensington. Richard Redgrave, head of the Department, submitted an artistic design that was considered worthy to adorn the capital's streets. In fact the design was short-lived, being cast by Smith and Hawkes between 1857 and 1859. Redgrave's box was a highly decorative affair. The hexagonal pillar was lavished with cast-iron

London's first letter box sited at the
corner of Fleet Street and Farringdon
Street, designed by A. E. Cowper and
made by H & M D Grissell of Hoxton,
1855. (*Post Office*)

facing page London letter box Number
2, a design that was superceded in 1857.
The instructions, as long as the postman's pillar hat is tall, were all too often
smeared with grime and manure to be as
useful as their length suggests. (*Post
Office*)

LONDON LETTER POST.

festoons of flowers and with Greek motifs around the underside of the shallow dome that capped it. However, a low-cost version of the Redgrave pillar box, shorn of garlands and festoons, was to inform the design of the standard pillar boxes which were to follow in 1859.

Redgrave did little to endear early British designers to bureaucrats, politicians and engineers. When the fulsome drawings of the ornamental boxes (now preserved in the Victoria and Albert Museum) were examined they revealed a small oversight on the designer's part. Almost unbelievably, Redgrave had forgotten to include a mouth for the letters to be dropped through. Because of the way in which the thickly-encrusted decoration was cast on the shaft of the pillar, it was impossible to add a mouth without destroying the look of the thing: the only solution was to cut an aperture in the top of the box. In practice this meant that rain poured down on the hapless mail. Artists soon proved to be very adept at designing postage stamps, but ever since the Redgrave affair the Post Office seems to have kept a wary eye on artistic designs for what is a very basic public utility.

A new design by E. A. Cowper, dating from 1859, was the result of wide-ranging discussions between the post masters of provincial districts. Certain key decisions were made that have lasted to this day. The mouth should in future be placed horizontally under the lip of the cap to protect letters from rain, sleet and snow, and there should be no superfluous decoration. The first batch of these new National Standard boxes, although only four feet tall, are strikingly similar to the type of pillar box that stayed in production for very nearly a century until the arrival of the K Type in 1979.

Nevertheless, nobody, least of all the policemen who were responsible for seeing that pillar boxes were not filled to overflowing, was particularly happy with the new National Standard design – mainly because it was too small. So in 1864 the architect and surveyor J. W. Penfold was employed by the Postmaster-General to come up with a new design. By popular demand Penfold returned to the early hexagonal profile. Penfold's

Suitably cautious approach to the richly-decorated London pillar box designed by the Department of Science and Art, South Kensington, in 1856. Two boxes survive in the hands of the Post Office Records. (*Crown Copyright*)

box, many of which still survive, became the standard issue box from 1866 until 1879, when the cylindrical style returned. Several changes were made over these thirteen years, but the basic design of this miniature Tower of the Winds remained intact. The key change was the decision to drop the mouth from immediately under the decorated cap to a position immediately above the door.

The return to the cylindrical form in 1879 followed long discussions over the question of the optimum shape for a pillar box. Both the Postmaster-General's office and the Office of Works agreed that, from an aesthetic point of view, the hexagon was infinitely superior to the cylindrical. However, it was also argued that letters were more easily trapped inside the Penfold box. The Office of Works began to press for a cylindrical box on grounds of ease of use, greater capacity within given overall dimensions, and ease of casting. The contract for the first of the new National Standard boxes was awarded to Handysides of Derby, well-known for the bridges and railways they had built in India and Russia. Distribution of the new design began in March 1879.

From the beginning there were two standard boxes, A and B, the former being much larger. The new National Standard pillar box of 1879 was the model for the boxes that were produced until the K type of 1979. In retrospect, it seems remarkable that one design could have lasted so long, but a good design remains a good design whether it was first produced in Victorian times or in the late 1970s. Whether the 1879 box was more or less good-looking than the Penfold box which preceded it is a wholly subjective matter. However, the functional superiority of the new box was never in dispute. The fact that the design changed so little over the next century was surely proof of that.

Just as the design of the pillar box was essentially fixed in 1879, so too was the colour. The first pillar boxes on Guernsey, dating from 1852, had been painted red, but district surveyors were then allowed to make up their own minds. Many were painted red, sometimes with the royal cipher picked out in gold; others were given a bronze

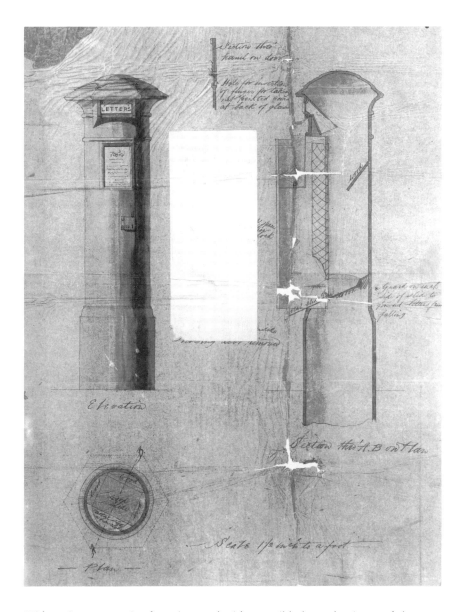

Without its cornucopia of cast iron and with a sensibly located, rain-proofed mouth, the London box of 1856 was adopted as the first National Standard in 1859. Several survive in Cork. (*Crown Copyright*)

finish, as was certainly the case with the decorative London boxes of 1857. However, to save confusion all pillar boxes were painted 'Bronze Green' in 1859. This was a dismal colour, and made the pillar box almost invisible in rural settings. A working example of a pillar box in this downbeat livery can be found in the subway that passes under the south pylon of Tower Bridge.

However, 'pillar box red' made its return in London from 1874. The move was by and large a functional one, ensuring that pillar boxes were visible from far away. The scarlet chosen was also particularly attractive. Boxes throughout the country followed suit and all were painted in the new style by 1884.

Since then various colour changes have been suggested. The first, chocolate brown, was temporarily adopted by two boxes in central London in 1887 because the standard red paint tended to fade all too quickly. Oddly enough, the Post Office was all in favour of the new colour, but luckily chocolate brown paint proved to be expensive to make, while improved colour-fast red dyes were on their way.

Other suggestions for different colours have been more fanciful. Red, white and blue was one patriotic suggestion; another was that luminous paint should be used so as to stop pedestrians from colliding with pillar boxes after hours. White was another possibility: it would surely prevent accidents after dark, but would hardly stand out against stone or stucco-faced buildings. The latest of these attempts to despoil Britain's pillar box dates from the 1970s, a decade already legendary for the appalling colours used in public sector design, of orange and brown interiors and garish orange, lime green and yellow street equipment. When the Type K box appeared in pillar box red at the beginning of the 1980s, the public sighed with relief.

Changes to the original design of 1879 came slowly but surely. In 1887 the royal Coat of Arms was restored to the standard box (its omission was nothing more than an administrative oversight, yet nothing was done until a formal complaint was registered by the grave Mr R. C. Toombs, Controller of the London Postal Service).

Graveyard of early letter boxes, showing from left to right, a rejected Smith & Hawkes fluted pillar of 1856, a decorative London box of 1857–9, one of the first London boxes of 1855–7, an early wall box and, on the ground, the decorative top of a standard Penfold pillar box of 1866–79. (*Post Office*)

The next major alteration was the repositioning of the mouth in the door of the box. The door itself was extended to the underlip of the cap, which made life much easier for postmen when collecting, since they no longer had to strain their back when grappling with letters stuck at the top of a box. This took place in 1904, the same year in which the words 'Next Collection' were cast into the box next to the time tablet (the little removable steel plate, now so rarely seen in our age of rampant vandalism).

The National Standard pillar box was occasionally under attack, not from vandals but from meddling officials who thought its design too plain. In 1912 the Postmaster-General asked the Board of Education to help with some new designs. The brief was passed on to the Royal College of Art and the students beavered away at producing a number of 'aesthetic designs'. Hexagonals and ovals were popular, as was superfluous decoration. The Office of Works was rightly critical, claiming that the National Standard was practical, rugged, easy to use and easy to clean. A fresh coat of paint every year kept up appearances. Although contractors were asked to prepare estimates for some of the new designs, the First World War interrupted any thoughts of meddling with new-fangled designs for pillar boxes. Suddenly there was more urgent work to be done.

One of the effects of the First World War in terms of design and architecture was the triumph of functionalism. After the carnage, a whole new generation of designers and architects, spurred on by the manifestoes of the Italian Futurists, by Le Corbusier's *Vers une Architecture*, and by the highly successful and highly functional machines invented during the war years, wanted to create a brave new Modern world. Ornament was crime. The new world was to be clear cut, white and clean. Buildings were to be stripped of all decoration. The aeroplane, that triumph of the functional aesthetic, pointed the way to clutter-free industrial design. In such an atmosphere any thoughts of decorating so functional an object as a pillar box – a public utility at that – would have been considered an outrage.

STANDARD LETTER BOXES.

The entire regiment of George V period
Standard Letter Boxes. (*Post Office*)

Yet what could be more functional than the National Standard pillar box of 1879? The cap with its residual fluting was there to keep off the rain, while the overall shape was exactly right for the task it had to perform. It could hardly have been criticised by even the most aggressive Modernist. Further changes were appropriately minimal. The mouth was enlarged again in 1957 to cope with the trend for ever larger envelopes. There was, however, a need for decorative change in 1954 after an unfortunate event which had occurred in Edinburgh two years earlier. In *The Letter Box*, Jean Farrugia recounts this tale of confused national identities following the installation of the first pillar box in Edinburgh to bear the cipher EIIR:

> Nothing untoward happened at the Edinburgh ceremony, but only thirty-six hours later it was discovered that the box had been daubed with tar. The reason why was soon made known to the Post Office. The cipher EIIR was quite unacceptable to the Scots because, it was declared, when used in Scotland, the title Elizabeth II is both historically incorrect and offensive. There had been no previous Scottish monarch of that name and moreover England's Elizabeth I was responsible for the execution of Mary, Queen of Scotland.

The upshot was that the Post Office decided to replace the royal cipher with a representation of the Scottish crown, but not before 'the offending EIIR pillar box on the Inch Housing estate had been blown up by a home-made bomb.'

The first and fortunately unsuccessful attempt to supplant the National Standard pillar box came in 1968 when David Mellor's bland rectangular box was erected outside St Paul's Cathedral. Manufactured by Vandyke Engineers of Harlow, the new box was meant to be revolutionary and to do away once and for all with the tried and trusted method of casting pillar boxes. The Mellor design was not cast, but instead it was composed of rectangular steel panels fixed to an internal steel frame. The design was meant to make life easier for postmen. Once it had been opened, a lever was pulled which shot the letters down into the waiting sack. Mellor argued that the square shape was a more natural one for envelopes, which makes some sense, but in terms of the contribution the new box made to the street scene, it was never going to be popular. Two hundred of the new boxes were made, but they were simply not tough enough for the job.

In 1974 the Carron Company was asked to see whether it would be possible to cast a rectangular box along Mellor's lines, but, thankfully for the British street, the experiment was unsatisfactory. The 1960s was the decade of *systems*: public housing was built using prefabricated building systems, and systems seemed to offer a rational way forward for modern design and architecture. However in practice tried and tested methods of construction often proved their superiority.

So when the Post Office returned to the idea of a new National Standard pillar box at the close of the 1970s, the new Type K was cylindrical and cast in iron.

Variations on a Theme

The Double Pillar Box

The vast increase in the volume of post carried throughout Britain following the adoption of Rowland Hill's Penny Post in 1840 soon placed a burden on the local postal districts. By the turn of the century the crying need was for a clear separation of town and country mail in busy urban districts. Accordingly, in 1896, a suggestion was made to the Postmaster-General by an Assistant Sub-Controller of the East London District that a new type of oval box should be cast, with separate mouths for 'town' and 'country'. The idea was taken up readily and Handysides of Derby was commissioned to cast the first double pillar box. Six boxes were tested in central London in 1898–9. They were an immediate success, and large orders followed. The new box was called the Type C and made its way into provincial towns from 1905.

In 1963 a very large number of Type Cs were cast for use elsewhere in London. Because this meant uprooting many old boxes, including a number of Penfold boxes dating back as early as 1866, conservationists suddenly realised that an undervalued part of Britain's heritage was about to disappear. This marked the beginning of the movement to conserve pillar boxes. Fortunately, the GPO decided to be helpful. Old Type A and Type B pillar boxes which had been supplanted by the oval Type Cs were stored in the old Woolwich Drill Hall, and either sold off to conservationists or else donated to local museums.

The arrival of the Type C also occasioned some talk as to whether separate mouths should be fitted low down on the roadside for the benefit of motorists. But, as Jean Farrugia notes, 'This suggestion has been repeated many times in recent years and in 1951 the introduction of two-way posting boxes for use for by both pedestrians and motorists (as used on the Continent) was again considered. However the objection to this type of box is that it would be likely to increase the risk of road accidents.'

The Type K of 1979 has been designed as a single pillar only. This has meant that, in central London at least, two boxes sometimes have to stand side by side to cope with town and country mail.

Air Mail Boxes
Air mail services began operation between London and Paris in 1919. Although the volume was low there was a demand from both business and the Post Office itself for a separate postal network. Consequently eleven air mail boxes were installed in central London as an experiment in 1930. These were normal Type Bs cast by the Carron Company, but painted blue and bearing white enamelled labels reading Air Mail. But although they attracted a good deal of welcome publicity, and proved that the GPO was up to the minute

By Command of the Postmaster General.

NOTICE to the PUBLIC.

Rapid Delivery of Letters.

GENERAL POST OFFICE,
May, 1849.

The Postmaster General is desirous of calling attention to the greater rapidity of delivery which would obviously be consequent on the general adoption of *Street-door Letter Boxes, or Slits,* in private dwelling houses, and indeed wherever the Postman is at present kept waiting.

He hopes that householders will not object to the means by which, at a very moderate expense, they may secure so desirable an advantage to themselves, to their neighbours, and to the Public Service.

Loquacious GPO notice heralding the arrival of the domestic letter box, 1849. (*Post Office*)

in catering for new developments, the blue boxes soon became redundant, since from 1936 letters to Europe could be treated as normal mail without even needing a distinctive Air Mail sticker. The service was extended throughout the Empire the following year, and talk of an entirely new type of Air Mail box was dropped.

The Telepill

The Telepill was not a medical means of keeping awake viewers new to television, but a hybrid machine that combined a post box, a pair of stamp-selling machines and a telephone engineer's cross-connection frame. The prototype Telepill was approved by the Royal Fine Art Commission, who claimed that it represented 'from an aesthetic point of view a definite advance in pillar box design'. A large and characterless rectangular cast-iron box, unveiled to cries of disbelief in 1947, this bulky monster was unacceptable to all but the most philistine local post offices and local authorities. It was quickly abandoned, and no more was said about it.

Signs

From as early as 1829 metal signs had directed the British public to the nearest Post Office. Such signs were not added to the tops of pillar boxes until 1924. However, when they did appear, every effort was made in their design not to upset the appearance of the host pillar box. The metal signs adopted were oval shaped, finished in cream with red lettering. Because of vandalism these are becoming increasingly rare.

Stamp machines

Demands for stamp-vending machines of one sort of another were made repeatedly by interested manufacturers and suppliers from the mid-1880s. A number of companies tried unsuccessfully to interest the Post Office in penny machines attached to pillar boxes that would dispense stamped post-cards and stamped letter paper that could be folded into an envelope and posted – so enabling people passing a pillar box to scribble a hurried message and post it immediately. In those days letters posted in a city even the size of London would arrive the same day, so this type of service was not something to sneeze at.

The Post Office, however, was unsure. If the machines failed, the public would inevitably blame the Post Office. However in 1891 the Post Office gave way and allowed trials of machines developed by the Stamp Distribution Syndicate Ltd. These served only to justify the Post Office's suspicions, in that they were unreliable and gave the public an opportunity to snipe at the Post Office.

It was only in the 1920s that the Post Office began to attach its own patent stamp-dispensing machines to the sides of pillar boxes. The boldest experiment it made along these lines was with the K4 telephone kiosk, designed by Giles Gilbert Scott, which incorporated a stamp-dispensing machine and a post box. This was erected outside St Michael's Church, Bath, and considered very successful. Fifty more were ordered in 1929 from the Carron Company.

The K4 was followed in 1932 by the Type D pillar box, an oval design with a built in stamp-vending machine. For various operational reasons Type D was considered awkward, and limited production ended the following year. But from 1933 machines were attached to selected pillar boxes. Again their disappearance from general use has been the result of theft and vandalism.

Lamp Boxes

Mostly found in rural areas, lamp boxes are small cast iron boxes attached to street lamps or telegraph poles. The first experiment with them was made in 1895, following American precedents. The lamp boxes served two useful functions: they were a cheap way of installing post boxes in rural areas, and they were made conspicuous by being lit up at night. Until the telephone became widely available people would often stop at a post box and scribble a quick line for instant mailing. A lamp to see by at night was considered a real boon for this purpose.

Wall Boxes

Less glamorous than pillar boxes, wall boxes have been in use since 1857 and have provided a low cost back-up service to pillar boxes. They are common features of rural Post Offices and did, in fact, revolutionise communications in the countryside. Pillar boxes were expensive to make and to install and for a while during the 1850s it looked as if villagers would have to remain out in the cold waiting for the arrival of the mail coach. The introduction of the wall box meant they could give up worrying about the coach.

Mass production began in 1858 and nine of the original 250 wall boxes are still in service, the most famous perhaps being at the Old Post Office, Tintagel, Cornwall. Although they boasted a handsome classical design resembling a foreshortened pilaster and bearing the royal cipher, the first boxes were soon considered unsatisfactory, since the casting allowed rainwater to drip into the box. Smith and Hawkes were commissioned to manufacture a new box, of which sixty survive up and down the country. These differ from the earliest boxes in having a higher door with the coats of arms set into it, as opposed to above it as in the 1858 model. A wire basket was incorporated inside, and a hood was moulded over the mouth to keep the rain at bay.

Modifications to what was a very straightforward functional design were many but relatively insignificant over the following century. Mouths had to be enlarged as the size of envelopes increased, and between 1959 and 1965 the Post Office carried out a nationwide programme of widening the mouths of Victorian and Edwardian wall boxes. Over five thousand boxes were so treated in the course of those six years, prolonging the life of old boxes indefinitely.

A few free-standing wall boxes were made during the reigns of Edward VII and George V. Only three are known to survive, even though they were of a particularly attractive design. The large rectangular boxes were topped with a small pyramidical roof surmounted with an elongated cast iron ball.

Until 1895 local postmasters were able to commission their own wall boxes. Up and down the country in small villages, where Post offices have survived 'rationalisation' (i.e. closure), you can still find Victorian wall boxes with elaborate lettering or else with bold enamel signs spelling out the legend 'Post Office Letter Box' in handsome late nineteenth-century display faces. Many of these boxes were made by James Ludlow of Birmingham, and are known as Ludlow Letter Boxes. The company continued to manufacture its non-standard boxes right up until it closed in 1965. The Ludlow boxes, although slowly disappearing from everyday use, can easily be distinguished by their enamel plates or, if these have been removed, by the lack of a rain hood over the aperture. They were made of sheet metal over wood, and so were more prone to rot than later standard issue cast iron wall boxes; as a result they are becoming difficult to find.

Occasionally special wall letter boxes were commissioned to harmonise with particular buildings. Until the 1960s what we now refer to as 'street furniture' was considered as part of the overall architectural fabric of the street, not as an appendage to add to the general clutter of the streetscape. The splendid bronze letter box set into the wall of Bentall's department store in Kingston-upon-Thames is a fine example of this fortunate meeting of noble building and public utility. The box, designed in a pseudo-Grecian style, harmonises well with the noble 'Wrennaissance' Edwardian shop.

Mobile Letter Boxes

Few people now remember the letter boxes that were once carried by buses and trams. The idea was first mooted in Dublin in 1889 and taken up by the London General Omnibus Company two years later. The LGOC suggested that buses stopping at the General Post Office in St-Martin's-le-Grand should be fixed with letter boxes for the benefit of both its passengers and the Post Office itself. The Post Office was unsure and wrote to the transport authorities in Paris who had been operating such a service for some years. Although reports from Paris were favourable, the Post Office hesitated.

Finally the Postmaster-General gave the go-ahead for a trial scheme in Huddersfield. Local trams were fitted with boxes in 1893 and proved to be a great success. The boxes fitted to the back of the tram were made of tin with brass doors painted red and stamped with the inscription 'Letter VR'. A penny surcharge was made for non-passengers who halted a tram simply to post a letter. Over the next twenty years the scheme was adopted by bus and tramway companies the length and breadth of Britain. The scheme was not always successful and appeared to depend on the vagaries of local conditions. It was, however, gradually extended until the outbreak of the Second World War, when it was officially abandoned. However, in a few special cases, especially in outlying rural areas, buses were allowed and even encouraged to carry post boxes. The Post Office itself began to operate its own bus services which carried passengers and mail in areas where normal commercial bus services could never be profitable. Some future privatisation of the Post Office would, of course, destroy these essential services overnight. Fortunately, the Post Office is still what it has been for many years, a public service and not a source of selfish profit-mongering.

Vandalism

Pillar boxes have been satisfying the nastier side of human nature since they made their first appearance. Fireworks, gunpowder and bombs have destroyed a number of boxes – or at least their contents – since Anthony Trollope's day. Penalties for interfering with the Royal Mail were severe – death or transportation for life – but even such drastic measures could not prevent pillar box crime. One of the earliest death sentences on record for stealing from a Post Office letter box was of a woman in Hanley, Newcastle-under-Lyme, in 1835.

Children were another nuisance. Victorian children were notably fond of dropping lighted matches into pillar boxes. This became such a nuisance that in 1895 a little boy was sentenced to be publicly whipped. The sentence was carried out and widely reported as a dire warning to the effect that the Post Office would stand no nonsense.

The Suffragettes had a particular dislike of pillar boxes. In early 1913 a concerted attack was made on pillar boxes in the revolutionary hot beds of Cheltenham, Beckenham and South Kensington. As Jean Farrugia records, 'oil of vitriol and suphuric acid was poured down the throats of the hapless victims.' Since then pillar boxes have been the hapless servants of terrorists and mindless thugs. Yet the pillar box's most persistent enemy is the dog. Try as it might in over a century the Post Office has found no way of preventing dogs from cocking their legs against pillar boxes.

Pillar boxes were often used in the days before the safety match for assisting in the lighting of pipes and cigarettes. The night watchman of Montrose was one such offender. However, he learnt to mend his ways one night in 1863. He struck a match against a particular pillar box as he had always done, but this petty misdemeanour was repaid with an almighty bang as the door of the letter box flew open in flames. According to the official report by the Postmaster-General, the explosion was caused by gas which had escaped from an adjacent street lamp during repairs made earlier that day and had bottled itself up inside the pillar box. The report did not mention the fate of the night watchman, but was 'pleased to report to Parliament that no letters had been damaged'.

Probably the most bizarre case of a pillar box being put out of action is recorded by Jean Farrugia:

Parliament was gravely informed by the Postmaster-General in his annual report of 1876, no-one could be found willing to undertake the task of emptying the wall letter box recently authorised for a village in the West of Ireland 'in a consequence of a general belief among the poorer people that, at that particular spot, a ghost went out nightly on parade.' The ghost was said to be a 'a large white turkey without a head'.

The pillar box's most aggressive assailants are the lorry and the car. Drivers of cars and lorries seem drawn towards pillar boxes as if they were giant red magnets set on the roadside, designed to cause accidents. Early Victorian pillar boxes do not disappear because of official vandalism, as people might want to believe, but because motorists, like dogs, seem unable to keep away from them.

The latest enemy is the 'tagger', those urchins who studiously avoid their homework in order to spray every possible surviving piece of public property with mindless graffiti. Pillar boxes are popular targets for 'taggers'. Perhaps they are really Young Conservatives with a mission to destroy faith in one of the last tolerably dignified public services?

The Future

Future policy is encouraging. Unlike British Telecom, the Post Office has no intention of destroying either its heritage or designs that are still performing the job they were intended for. Pillar boxes have been, for the most part, designed to last, and despite one or two unfortunate experiments in design and colour, the red pillar box seems destined to survive long into the future. The K Type box of 1979 will slowly make itself better known, but only as and when a new pillar box is really needed.

Casting a Pillar Box

Most pillar boxes have been cast in iron. This age-old method guarantees a remarkably strong and enduring public servant that is expected to last at least a hundred years and in practice can last much longer. Jean Farrugia waxes lyrical about the actual casting process. 'No one,' she has written in *The Letter Box*, 'who has been present at the casting of a pillar box could, I feel sure, ever feel quite the same about letter boxes ... words cannot express the mounting excitement as the moment of casting draws near.' So how is a pillar box made?

A National Standard pillar box was cast in four separate pieces – base, cylinder, door and cap. Red-hot molten iron was poured into a moulding box at the foundry, spreading across the metal patterns. After the casting had cooled, it was removed from the moulding and smoothed down laboriously by hand. The four pieces were then attached together and the completed pillar box painted and made ready for delivery. The base of the box extended some way down into the ground to ensure that it stood upright. However as British city streets, and London's in particular, are continually being dug up, filled and dug up again for the provision of more and more cables and servicing, pillar boxes are hard pressed to remain vertical.

Designing a New Pillar Box: The Type K, 1979
Patterns for various types of National Standard boxes were beginning to wear out by the late 1970s. This meant that new pillar boxes became increasingly difficult to make, while existing ones were expensive to repair. Fifty or a hundred years of door-slamming by postmen in a hurry had caused cracks in hundreds of cast iron doors. So the Post Office decided to commission a brand new design in 1978.

Tony Gibbs of Hop Studios was duly commissioned by Barry Robinson, the Post Office's Design Co-ordinator, and the first of four hundred K Type boxes were cast at the Lion Foundry of Kirkintilloch in Scotland a year later, exactly a century after the first cylindrical National Standard pillar box.

Various materials were considered for the new design, including fabricated steel, shell concrete and glass-reinforced plastic, but fortunately none of these proved to be as tough or as vandal-resistant as traditional cast iron. After discussions with the Lion Foundry and David Poulton, the Post Office Chief Engineer, Gibbs set to work on the drawing-board. The design was agreed at a very early stage.

The K Type was meant to be a simplification of the old National Standards. The reason for this was not some anti-decorative lobby in the Post Office, but a decision to reduce damage to new pillar boxes both in the foundry and on the way to their allotted sites. Royal ciphers standing proud of the old pillar boxes had often been damaged as they were rolled across the foundry floor, and again during delivery. Gibbs set the new E I I R cipher back in a sloping recessed panel. By doing this, and by designing a new rainwater gutter that dispensed with the traditional pillar box cap, he created a box that could be rolled across the foundry floor without damage.

The sloping inset panel was not designed simply to make the casting and transport process safer and simpler than it had been previously, but also to incorporate a new times of collection panel. Postmen and Post Office engineers agreed that a sloping panel would be easier to read, saving the public from having to stoop down. Behind its mild steel door, the K Type is very different from its predecessors. Letters filter through a 'fish mouth' chute that makes it impossible to fish letters out from the outside. They then fall into a plastic mesh basket and enter the postman's sack through a sloping chute at the base.

The K Type is lifted onto its side by a crane mounted on a lorry, which is why you can see a few examples crowned with circular steel rings: these are meant to be removed on delivery, and the gap filled with a brass plug, but this has not always been done. Other K Types have a Post Office direction sign screwed into their tops – a new version of the enamel oval plate. Cast in aluminium, the plate employs the new Post Office lettering designed by Banks & Miles. Originally Tony Gibbs wanted these painted red with the paint on the cast letters polished away so that they stood out in silver on a red background, but instead they are yellow, slavishly following the Banks & Miles Post Office corporate design manual.

The K Type proved to be relatively difficult to cast. The rainwater gutter required a separate casting, while craftsmen have had to work meticulously to achieve the smooth finish dictated by the form of the box. The rejection rate at the Lion Foundry was initially high. Nevertheless the first K Type was installed outside the Albert Hall within twelve months of the commission being approved. The Gibbs box has proved to be successful, although as yet no twin 'town' and 'country' version exists. The new box will only replace existing boxes if these are found to be beyond repair.

Pillar Box Number 1, Union Street, St
Peter Port, Guernsey, the end product
of Anthony Trollope's historic report
on the need for roadside letter boxes.
This classically inspired pillar is still in
everyday use. Note the odd coat of
arms: the unicorn, for some unknown
reason, has chosen to face away from
the lion. (*Crown copyright*)

Early mainland letterboxes based on the Channel Island design. As local postmasters were able to commission their own designs at this date (c.1856) there are detail differences between these two boxes. The box on the *left* cast by John Butt & Co of Gloucester can be seen located at Barnes Cross, Bishops Caundle, Dorset. The one on the *right* can be found in Framlingham, Suffolk. The details of this box are far more refined. (*Post Office*)

38

facing page This is the pillar box designed for use in London by the Department of Science and Art, South Kensington in 1856. In their lust for decorative effect, the Kensington aesthetes forgot to include a letter mouth. As is evident, this had to be cut into the cap after casting by Messrs Smith & Hawkes. A hinged flap was added later to keep the rain out. (*Post Office*).

left The cast iron base was set deep into the London clay to ensure stability. (*Post Office*)

facing page The Kensington box was adapted for use by A. E. Cowper at low cost elsewhere in the country. This Berkshire box survived until recent times.

The Cowper box, the first National Standard of 1859–66 was cast by a number of ironfounders and so there were a number of detail differences between batches of the new design both inside and out. The box on the *right* stood originally in Portland Road, Newcastle-upon-Tyne. The one on the *left* is now in the care of Exeter City Museum. (*Post Office*)

Non-standard fluted pillar boxes
designed by Mr Edge and cast by Smith
& Hawkes, 1856–60. Both these de-
lightful boxes survive, in Banbury,
Oxfordshire (*left*) and in Eton High
Street, Berkshire (*right*). (*Post Office*)

Fluted pillar boxes at collection time.
Left, Banbury (seen in 1968) and *right*
in Oxford Street, Bilsten, Birmingham.
(*Post Office; Crown Copyright*)

43

44

A parade of non-standard Victorian pillar boxes all dating from *c*.1856. From left to right: a local box of unknown design and origin that once stood in Kilmarnock (*Crown Copyright*); a special and regal Liverpool box designed by Mr Gay, District Surveyor, 1863, based on A. E. Cowper's version of the decorative Kensington box (*Post Office*); unique floriated box dating from *c*.1860 that once stood in St George's Square, Pimlico (*Post Office*); one of Mr Edge's rejected designs – a fluted box capped with a bell-shaped dome and crown (*Crown Copyright*); another obscure Scottish box used by an Aberdeen granite firm for over seventy years and now owned by the Post Office (*Crown Copyright*).

Two examples of J. W. Penfold's highly successful National Standard box, based on the Athenian Tower of the Winds, cast by Cochrane & Co, 1866–79. The box on the *right* with the lower set mouth has since been recovered from its old setting – Lovaine Crescent, New-castle-upon-Tyne – photographed there in 1907. (*Post Office*)

facing page Penfold box adorning and complementing the London streetscape. Cornwall Gardens, Kensington, 1989. (*Author*)

above, left and right Posting letters the
Penfold way, Buxton, Derbyshire, 1935.
(*Post Office*)

facing page Postman's view of a Penfold
box. (*Post Office*)

48

49

Penfold details: the decorative cap was effective in keeping rain at bay. The coat of arms cast immediately under the cap is gradually disappearing under layers of fresh paint. Queen Victoria's cipher is centred on the door. The relationship of the various elements to one another – cap, coat of arms, mouth and timetable – is particularly satisfying. (*Author*)

Collections

Monday to Friday

1	09.15	3	15.45
2	13.30	4	17.30

Later collection at SWDO MLO 53 Nine Elms
Lane London SW8 5BB 21.00

Saturday

		1	09.30
		2	12.00

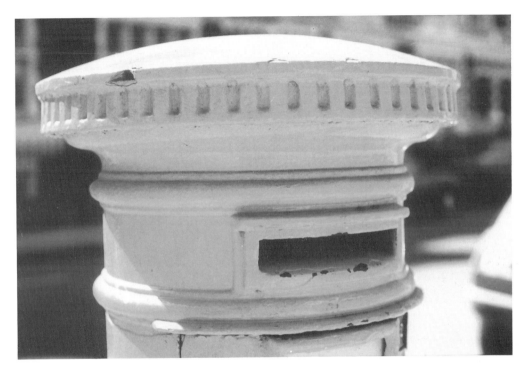

facing page Early National Standard
Type A, adopted by the Post Office in
1879. This version on duty in Nevern
Square (*left*), London s w 5 has the
mouth set very high and lacks a royal
cipher. The mouth was set lower in
following years, while the royal cipher
made a return. Both these features can
be seen on this Type A box in Bramham
Gardens, London s w 5 . (*Author*)

above One of the smaller Victorian
Type B boxes. Earl's Court, London
s w 5 . (*Author*)

facing page A recently cast Penfold box painted in the short lived Victorian olive green and gold in the shadow of Tower Bridge. Letters can be posted here. (*Author*)

above National Standard pillar boxes can still be found in everyday use throughout former British colonies and dependencies. This Victorian box (*left*) waves the flag in Hong Kong. A handsome Edwardian Type A displaying its florid royal cipher and topped with an oval signpost indicating the nearest Post Office (*right*) – Portland Place, London W1, 1952. (*Post Office*)

facing page Contrast in royal ciphers: Edward VII's cipher is seen *left*, while Edward VIII's cipher (*right*) is rarely seen at all. Note that the legend 'Post Office' was now added below the cipher. As they moved further into the twentieth century National Standard pillar boxes became more decorated, not less as might be expected. (*Author*)

right One of the very few Edward VIII boxes can be found here in West Temple Sheen, London s w 1 4. (*Author*)

A fully equipped Edward VII Type A with back-packing stamp machine and topped with one of the elegant, but rapidly vanishing, Post Office direction signs. In this instance in Castelnau, Hammersmith, London W6, the Post Office is about six feet away. (*Author*)

One of the special and short lived
George V Air Mail boxes erected in
1935. The first to be erected and the last
to be recovered was this one in King
Edward Street, London E C 1. (*Post
Office*)

One of the first Elizabeth II boxes (*left*). This Type A was sited in Horse Guard's Parade, Whitehall. Note the frequency of letter collections in 1952. This standard George VI Type B (*right*) is coupled to a contemporary penny post stamp machine, since removed or replaced on all boxes. (*Post Office*)

The 'Town' and 'Country' Type C made its appearance in central London at the very end of Queen Victoria's reign. This one (*facing page, left*) is in Moorgate, London E C 1 . (*Facing page right, and above*) in the same street stands this George V example. By this time the royal cipher had been moved from the doors on either side of the box to a more conspicuous position on the front. (*Author*)

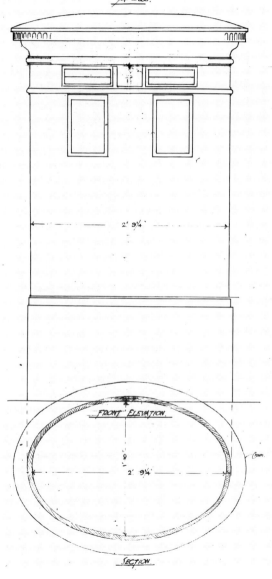

PILLAR LETTER BOX
TYPE 'C' (DOUBLE)
¼ Size.

2' 9¼"

FRONT ELEVATION.

2' 9¼"

Crown.

SECTION.

Original drawing by Post Office engineers for Type C 'Town' and 'Country' box. (*Post Office*)

facing page Two versions of Georgian Type C's: *left*, a standard George VI box designated for London's Bedford Square (twelve collections a day); *right*, a George V box incorporating a stamp machine. (*Post Office*)

Contrast between the sheet-metal Type F designed by David Mellor, seen here in front of St Paul's Cathedral in 1968 (*facing page, left*), and the slab-sided Type G, a revision based on the same design but tougher – and cruder. This example (*facing page, right*) is in Queen's Gate, Kensington. The ingenious interior mechanism (*left*), designed by David Mellor, was common to both designs.

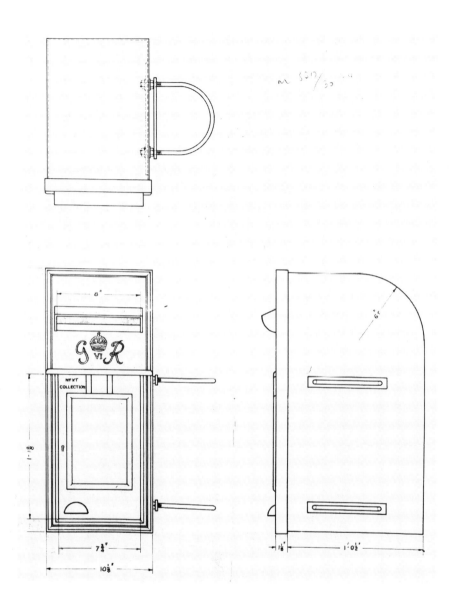

This type of George VI letter box was
designed to be attached to trams. This
service ended in 1939. (*Post Office*)

George VI lamp-post letter box. (*Post Office*)

Victorian wall box seen on a wall in St
Mary's, Isle of Scilly. *(Post Office)*

Wall boxes came in a variety of guises. This Victorian box (*left*) is an example from the Lake District. Describing this George VI design from Stapleford Abbots, Essex as a 'lamp box' seems a bit of a misnomer, but that is what it is. (*Post Office*)

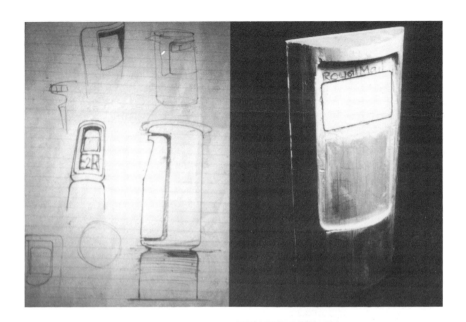

The making of the Type K: (*left*), early
design sketches and rough working
model; (*right*), Tony Gibb's finished
coloured drawing. The design was
finalised at a very early stage. (*Design
Council*)

facing page Type K letter box designed
by Tony Gibbs in 1978 – first per-
formed outside the Albert Hall the
following year. (*Author*)

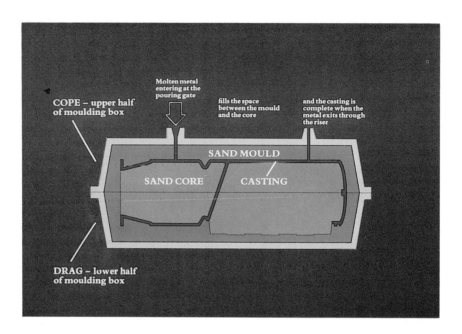

Diagram of the mould in which the
Type K is cast. (*Design Council*)

facing page New pillar box emerging
from its cast (*left*); front section of the
cast showing the E I I R royal cipher
(*right*). (*Design Council*)

When cast the surface of each box has
to be filed and sandpapered to a fine
finish before painting. (*Design Council*)

Post office direction sign designed by
Tony Gibbs to complement the Type
K. (*Design Council*)

APPENDIX

Where to Find Old and Rare Letter Boxes

A list of old and rare pillar, wall and lamp boxes would be far too long to include in this book. However, the Letter Box Study Group is able to help. The Group still needs help in sleuthing down rare boxes so that it can provide at some time in the future a comprehensive gazetteer of the British letter box. Nevertheless it might only be fair to list some of the rare examples mentioned in the text and to point out towns in which the oldest and most interesting can be found on many street corners.

The earliest of all boxes, the Vaudin pillar box of 1852–5, can be found at:
Bristol South Western Regional Post Office Headquarters – Bond Street
St Peter Port, Guernsey – Union Street

Early Mainland (1853–6):
Bishop's Caundle (Dorset) – Barnes Cross, Holwell
Plymouth – Royal Naval Hospital, Stonehouse

Early Mainland (1856–60):
Gosberton (Lincs) – Sutterton Road
Framlingham, Suffolk – Double Street, Saxtead Road

Fluted (from 1856); vertical posting aperture:
Banbury – Bridge Street
Birkenhead – Palm Grove/Devonshire Road
Gravesend – Norfolk Road/St John's Road
Milford-on-Sea – Cornwallis Road/Victoria Road
Christchurch – Mudeford Quay
Warwick – Eastgate, Westgate
Windsor – Eton High Street

Fluted (from 1860); horizontal posting aperture:
Malvern – Orchard Road, St Andrew's Road, Worcester Road
Solihull – Dog Kennel Lane

Economy version of London's ornate boxes designed by Richard Redgrave can still be found in Cork, Eire.

First National Standards (1859–66) are still quite common in Liverpool. Otherwise they can only be found in:
Aberdeen – Ferryhill Post Office
Brighton – Montepelier Road
Portsmouth – World's End, Hambledon
Purley – Foxley Lane/Furze Lane

Liverpool Specials, 1863:
Liverpool 6 – Sheil Road/Huntley Road
Liverpool 6 – Brech Road/Everton
Road
Liverpool 13 – Church Road/Edge Lane

Hexagonal Penfolds are still quite
common, and are scattered across
Britain and Eire. There is a large
gathering in Cheltenham, three each in
Manchester and Oxford, and a large
colony in the old inner suburbs of
London.

National Standard cylindrical boxes
dating from the earliest period, 1879–83,
are common. The largest clans can be
found in Bootle, Brighton, Cambridge,
Eastbourne, Liverpool and the old inner
London suburbs.

Other early examples can be found in
the National Postal Museum Collection,
King Edward Building, King Edward
Street. London E C 1 – (the pillar box
collection can be seen by appointment
only) – as well at the following local
museums:
Lukis Museum, St Peter Port,
Guernsey, Channel Islands
Salford Art Gallery & Museum, Peel
Park, Salford 5
Exeter City Museum, Devon
Worthing Museum, Sussex
Glasgow Art Gallery & Museum
Rochdale Museum, Lancs
Guildhall Museum, Windsor, Berks
Aykley Heads Folk Museum, Barnard
Castle, Co. Durham
Bankfield Museum, Halifax, Yorkshire
Chiddingstone Castle, Edenbridge,
Kent
Dudley Art Gallery & Museum, Worcs
Norfolk Castle Museum
The Museum of London, Barbican,
E.C.1.
Carnegie Library, Herne Hill, S.E.4.
Walthamstow Vestry House Museum,
E.17.

BIBLIOGRAPHY

Books on letter boxes are as rare as some of the earlier pillar boxes themselves. The seminal book on the subject is Jean Farrugia Young, *The Letter Box* (Centaur Press, 1969).

Specialist publications:
Martin Robinson, *Old Letter Boxes* (Shire Publications, 1987).
Martin Robinson, *A Guide to Rare British Letter Boxes* (Letter Box Study Group, second edition, 1988).

General Books on Post Office History:
Herbert Joyce, *The History of the Post Office from its establishment down to 1836* (Richard Bentley & Son, 1893).
Howard Robinson, *Britain's Post Office* (Oxford University Press, 1953).
Sir Rowland Hill and George Birbeck Hill, *The Life of Sir Rowland Hill and the History of the Penny Postage* (Thos de la Rue & Co, 1880).
Edmund Vale, *The Mail Coach men of the late Eighteenth Century* (David & Charles, 1967).
Jean Farrugia and Tony Gammons, *Carrying British Mails: Five Centuries of Postal Transport by Land, Sea and Air* (National Postal Museum).

Information Sheets on various aspects of Post Office history are available free of charge from Post Office Archives, Freeling House, 23 Glasshill Street, London SE1 0BQ. These include:

1. Pillar Boxes 1852–1964: an Illustrated History.
2. Victorian Pillar Boxes: List (1969).
3. Edward VIII Pillar Boxes: List (1969).

Up to date lists are available from the Letter Box Study Group, c/o 43 Miall Road, Hall Green, Birmingham BS28 9BS. Information from the Letter Box Study Group will save thwarted journeys. Early or rare pillar boxes do still disappear, although all are now listed.